Rhymers` Club

The second book of the Rhymers' Club

Rhymers' Club

The second book of the Rhymers' Club

ISBN/EAN: 9783337259419

Printed in Europe, USA, Canada, Australia, Japan

Cover: Foto ©Andreas Hilbeck / pixelio.de

More available books at **www.hansebooks.com**

THE SECOND BOOK

OF

THE RHYMERS' CLUB

LONDON: ELKIN MATHEWS & JOHN LANE
NEW YORK: DODD, MEAD & COMPANY
1894

J. MILLER AND SON, PRINTERS, EDINBURGH

THE RHYMERS' CLUB

ERNEST DOWSON
EDWIN J. ELLIS
G. A. GREENE
ARTHUR CECIL HILLIER
LIONEL JOHNSON
RICHARD LE GALLIENNE
VICTOR PLARR
ERNEST RADFORD
ERNEST RHYS
T. W. ROLLESTON
ARTHUR SYMONS
JOHN TODHUNTER
W. B. YEATS

Some of the following Poems have been published in various periodicals, *The Academy*, *The National Observer*, *The Spectator*, *The Bookman*, *Macmillan*, *The Hobby-Horse*, etc.; others again in *A Fellowship in Song*, in *Book-Song*, and in *A Light Load*. We are indebted to the various Editors for courteous permission to republish.

CONTENTS

IN WESTMINSTER ABBEY

October 12, 1892

In her still House of Fame her Laureate dead
England entombs to-day, lays him to rest,
The leaves of honour green around his head,
Love's flowers fresh on his breast.

Mourn him in solemn service of high song,
Music serene as breathed in his last breath,
When, to the soundless ocean borne along,
He met majestic Death.

Mourn him with grief's most fair solemnities,
Ritual that with an inward rapture suits,
While in stern pomp the mind's grave companies
March, as to Dorian flutes.

A

If tears we shed, 'tis but as eyes grow dim
  When some rich strain superbly rolls away,
For like the close of an Olympian hymn
    Ended his golden day.

Bear him in pride, like a dead conqueror
  Brought home to his last triumph in sad state,
Over him his Country's Flag, who in life's war
    Was victor over fate.

We saw him stand, a lordly forest tree,
  His branches filled with music, all the air
Glad for his presence; fallen at last is he,
    And all the land is bare.

So, with old Handel thundering in our ears,
  His mighty dirge marching from breast to breast
In sorrow's purple pageant, with proud tears
    We leave him to his rest.

JOHN TODHUNTER.

BEYOND?

WHAT lies beyond the splendour of the sun,
  Beyond his flashing belt of sister-spheres?
  What deeps are they whereinto disappears
The visitant comet's sword, of fire fine-spun?

What rests beyond the myriad lights that run
  Their nightly race around our human fears?
  Hope-signals raised on multitudinous spears
Of armies captained by the Eternal One?

Beyond the sun, and far beyond the stars,
  Beyond the weariness of this our day,
Beyond this fretting at the prison-bars,
  The urgent soul, divine in soulless clay,
Bids us set forth, through endless avatars,
  To seek where God hath hidden Himself away.

G. A. GREENE.

AD CINERARIUM

WHO in this small urn reposes,
Celt or Roman, man or woman,
Steel of steel, or rose of roses ?

Whose the dust set rustling slightly,
In its hiding-place abiding,
When this urn is lifted lightly ?

Sure some mourner deemed immortal
What thou holdest and enfoldest,
Little house without a portal !

When the artificers had slowly
Formed thee, turned thee, sealed thee, burned thee,
Freighted with thy burden holy,

Sure, he thought, 'there's no forgetting
All the sweetness and completeness
Of such rising, of such setting,'

And so bade them grave no token,
Generation, age, or nation,
On thy round side still unbroken,—

Let them score no cypress verses,
Funeral glories, prayers, or stories,
Mourner's tears, or mourner's curses,

Round thy brown rim time hath polished;—
Left thee dumbly cold and comely
As some shrine of gods abolished.

Ah 'twas well! It scarcely matters
What is sleeping in the keeping
Of this house of mortal tatters,—

Steel of steel, or rose of roses,
Man or woman, Celt or Roman,
If but soundly he reposes!

VICTOR PLARR.

EXTREME UNCTION

Upon the lips, the eyes, the feet,
  On all the passages of sense,
The atoning oil is spread with sweet
  Renewal of lost innocence.

The feet that lately ran so fast
  To meet desire, are soothly sealed:
The eyes, that were so often cast
  On vanity, are touched and healed.

From troublous sights and sounds set free,
  In such a twilight hour of breath,
Shall one retrace his life, or see
  Through shadows the true face of Death?

Vials of mercy! sacring oils!
  I know not where, nor when I come,
Nor through what wanderings and toils
  To crave of you Viaticum.

Yet when the walls of flesh grow weak,
  In such an hour, it well may be,
Through mist and darkness light shall break,
  And each anointed sense shall see!

ERNEST DOWSON.

SOLACE

(*In Memoriam W. H. W.*)

He worketh still.
Superior to Death's smart
He worketh still.
What his spent years could not fulfil
I shall endeavour for my part:
For ever, living in my heart,
He worketh still.

Ernest Radford.

LOST

Something has gone.
Oh life, great giver as thou art,
Something has gone.
Not love, for love as years roll on
Plays evermore a fuller part.
But of the treasure of my heart
Something has gone.

Ernest Radford.

MYSTIC AND CAVALIER

Go from me: I am one of those, who fall.
What! hath no cold wind swept your heart at all,
In my sad company? Before the end,
        Go from me, dear my friend!

Yours are the victories of light: your feet
Rest from good toil, where rest is brave and sweet:
But after warfare in a mourning gloom,
        I rest in clouds of doom.

Have you not read so, looking in these eyes?
Is it the common light of the pure skies,
Lights up their shadowy depths? The end is set:
        Though the end be not yet.

When gracious music stirs, and all is bright,
And beauty triumphs through a courtly night;
When I too joy, a man like other men:
        Yet, am I like them, then?

And in the battle, when the horsemen sweep
Against a thousand deaths, and fall on sleep:
Who ever sought that sudden calm, if I
        Sought not? yet could not die!

Seek with thine eyes to pierce this crystal sphere:
Canst read a fate there, prosperous and clear?
Only the mists, only the weeping clouds,
        Dimness and airy shrouds.

Beneath, what angels are at work? What powers
Prepare the secret of the fatal hours?
See! the mists tremble, and the clouds are stirred:
        When comes the calling word?

The clouds are breaking from the crystal ball,
Breaking and clearing: and I look to fall.
When the cold winds and airs of portent sweep,
        My spirit may have sleep.

O rich and sounding voices of the air!
Interpreters and prophets of despair:
Priests of a fearful sacrament! I come,
        To make with you mine home.

LIONEL JOHNSON.

THE ROSE IN MY HEART

All things uncomely and broken, all things worn out and old,
The cry of a child by the roadway, the creak of a lumbering cart,
The heavy steps of the ploughman splashing the winter mould,
Are wronging your image that blossoms a rose in the deeps of my heart.

The wrong of the things misshapen is wrong too great to be told;
I hunger to build them anew, and sit on a green knoll apart,
With the earth, and the sky, and the water, re-made like a casket of gold
For my dreams of your image that blossoms a rose in the deeps of my heart.

W. B. Yeats.

HOWEL THE TALL

I

HAWK of war, Howel the Tall,
 Prince of men :
Dead is Howel, David slew him;
He will not lead to war again !

Periv once, Kedivor's son,
 Sang him so,
Sang his youth and death and passion,
Now nine centuries ago.

But they say—the bardic poets,
 In their tales :
Whoso names in rhyme those heroes,
Calls them back again to Wales :

Calls them back, and gives them there
 Life and breath
In the grey and ancient places,
Where they gave their hearts to Death.

And this broken rhyme is made
For a spell,
From the shades to summon Howel
To the land he loved so well.

II

Owain loved an Irish princess :
So there sprang
Howel of two passionate races,
When harp and sword in Argoed rang.

Owain Gwyned, golden sire
Of seven sons,
Fathered him: when Death took Owain,
Seven claimed the crown at once.

First-born of the seven, blighted
Yorweth came;
Then David of the dagger-stroke,
And Madoc of the sailor's fame.

David's fingers felt the crown,
And he said,
'Yorweth of the broken face;—
Ere he reign, be David dead!'

Blighted Yorweth might not reign,
        Wanting grace:
Then the swords rang out for Howel,
For the beauty of his face.

Hawk of war! Howel ruled them
        Royally:
But his mother's blood was in him;
One morn he sailed the Irish Sea.

O, high the Gaelic welcome
        Of her house,
When he stayed to share the feasting
At their Lammas-tide carouse.

All too long indeed, while David,
        Left at home,
Plied Argoed with fine fury—
'Base-born Howel well may roam:

'Not for me this bastard bred
        Shall be King,
To come anon with Irishry
Of his mother's nurturing:

'Out my sword!' As swift the word,
        Winged with fate,
Over sea was sped to Howel:—
Come, or yet it be too late!

Through the night the horsemen came,
        Spurring west:
'Hawk of war, arouse! the ravens
Pick to shreds your mountain nest!'

Howel's horn broke up the feast:
        All the night
They galloped thro' the Gadael's fields,
And reached the sea at morning light.

As he rode, at Howel's heart
        Stirred the strain,
That he sang them while they waited
For the ship to Porth Dinlleyn.

HOWEL'S SONG

A foaming wave flows o'er the grave
        Where Rhivawn lies;
Ah, I love the land beyond Arvon,
Where the trefoil grows and the mountains rise.

I love at eve the seaward stream
        Where the seamews brood,
And the famous vale of Cwm Dythore,
Where the nightingale sings in the privet wood.

I love the land where we drank the mead,
        And drove the spear,
At the forest side of Tegenyl,
Where my yellow steed outdid the deer;

Where Hunyd's love, and Gwen's white arm,
        Defend my doom;
Where Olwen is, and Gwenerys,
And Nesta like the apple-bloom!

A foaming wave cried out all night
        Upon my fate;
Last night I dreamt of an open grave,
A crying wound, and a closing gate.

A foaming wave flows o'er the grave
        Of Rhivawn's sleep:
But dig my grave at the forest side,
Where the trefoils grow, and the squirrels leap!

III

There sang the heart whose even-song
Came too true,
That soon lay rent on Arvon field
By David's dagger through and through.

Dead is the Prince of Chivalry;
But Kymric rhyme
May call him yet to Argoed,
'Tis said, as of old time.

The shepherd there, at nightfall,
O'er his sheep
Humming some old warlike rhyme,
May see him cross the steep.

There, late I climbed from Cwm Dythore
The triple height,
To wait beside the mountain cairn
The ancient mystery of night.

The mountain drew his purple robe
Around,
And his seven tireless torrents
Sent from the Cwm a lonely sound.

From the haunted vale of Howel
At my feet,
I surely heard his even-song
Rise mountain-wild and sweet?—

'I love at eve the seaward stream,
Where the seamews brood;
And the famous vale of Cwm Dythore,
Where the nightingale sings in the privet wood!'

And surely here, beside the cairn,
A shadowy form
Gazes afar on Arvon field,
Where the cottage fires shine warm?

His mien heroic, round his brow
The circling bay;
Around his neck the golden torque
Finds his dark locks half-way?

* * * * *

So come the stars, so come and go,
And he was gone;
Poised high, amid the mountain-night,
Beneath the stars, I stood alone.

But down the track the shepherds take,
    As I clung
On the torrent's brink, benighted,
And the mountain-fox gave tongue—

Night, nor Time, nor David's dagger,
    Could give pause
To your deathless rhyme, O Howel,
And, O Wales, your ancient cause!

Ernest Rhys.

A BALLAD OF LONDON

AH, London! London! our delight,
Great flower that opens but at night,
Great City of the midnight sun,
Whose day begins when day is done.

Lamp after lamp against the sky
Opens a sudden beaming eye,
Leaping alight on either hand,
The iron lilies of the Strand.

Like dragonflies, the hansoms hover,
With jewelled eyes, to catch the lover,
The streets are full of lights and loves,
Soft gowns, and flutter of soiled doves.

The human moths about the light
Dash and cling close in dazed delight,
And burn and laugh, the world and wife,
For this is London, this is life!

Upon thy petals butterflies,
But at thy root, some say, there lies,
A world of weeping trodden things,
Poor worms that have not eyes or wings.

From out corruption of their woe
Springs this bright flower that charms us so,
Men die and rot deep out of sight
To keep this jungle-flower bright.

Paris and London, World-Flowers twain
Wherewith the World-Tree blooms again,
Since Time hath gathered Babylon,
And withered Rome still withers on.

Sidon and Tyre were such as ye,
How bright they shone upon the tree!
But Time hath gathered, both are gone,
And no man sails to Babylon.

Ah, London! London! our delight,
For thee, too, the eternal night,
And Circe Paris hath no charm
To stay Time's unrelenting arm.

RICHARD LE GALLIENNE.

VENUS

UNSEEN forever, save by her own boy—
  And he is love, the ever blind and young,
  Blind by the light of his own youth out-flung—
Venus, the daughter of the whole world's joy,
Whom wisdom cannot hide nor years annoy,
  Like the bright sea whereout her birth is sprung,
  Still dances to her praise for ever sung,
And lives to laugh, to save and to destroy.
  But now, some say, she has returned again,
Being unseen, to her deep sleep in bliss.
  No, no ; while there are women loved of men,
As this is loved—and this is loved—and this—
  Venus returns no more beneath the sea :
  Seek her not there, for this—and this is she.

EDWIN J. ELLIS.

NORA ON THE PAVEMENT

As Nora on the pavement
Dances, and she entrances the grey hour
Into the laughing circle of her power,
The magic circle of her glances,
As Nora dances on the midnight pavement;

Petulant and bewildered,
Thronging desires and longing looks recur,
And memorably re-incarnate her,
As I remember that old longing,
A footlight fancy, petulant and bewildered;

There where the ballet circles,
See her, but ah, not free her from the race
Of glittering lines that link and interlace ;
This colour now, now that, may be her,
In the bright web of those harmonious circles.

But what are these dance measures,
Leaping and joyous, keeping time alone
With life's capricious rhythm, and all her own,
Life's rhythm and hers, long sleeping,
That wakes, and knows not why, in these dance
measures?

It is the very Nora;
Child, and most blithe, and wild as any elf,
And innocently spendthrift of herself,
And guileless and most unbeguiled,
Herself at last, leaps free the very Nora.

It is the soul of Nora,
Living at last, and giving forth to the night,
Bird-like, the burden of its own delight,
All its desire, and all the joy of living,
In that blithe madness of the soul of Nora.

ARTHUR SYMONS.

MORNING

CYCLING SONG

In the airy whirling wheel is the springing strength of steel
And the sinew grows to steel day by day,
Till you feel your pulses leap at the easy swing and sweep
As the hedges flicker past upon the way.
Then it's out to the kiss of the morning breeze,
And the rose of the morning sky,
And the long brown road where the tired spirit's load
Slips off as the leagues go by.

Black and silver, swift and strong, with a pleasant undersong
From the steady rippling murmur of the chain—

Half a thing of life and will, you may feel it start and thrill
With a quick elastic answer to the strain
As you ride to the kiss of the morning breeze,
And the rose of the morning sky,
And the long brown road where the tired spirit's load
Slips off as the leagues go by.

Miles a hundred you may run from the rising of the sun
To the gleam of the first white star;
You may ride through twenty towns, meet the sun upon the downs
Or the wind on the mountain scaur.
Then it's out to the kiss of the morning breeze,
And the rose of the morning sky,
And the long brown road where the tired spirit's load
Slips off as the leagues go by.

Down the pleasant country side, through the woodland's summer pride
You have come in your forenoon spin—
And you never would have guessed how delicious is the rest
In the shade by the wayside inn,

When you've sought the kiss of the morning breeze,
And the rose of the morning sky,
And the long brown road where the tired spirit's load
Slips off as the leagues go by.

Oh, there's many a one who teaches that the shining river reaches
Are the place to spend a long June day.
But give me the whirling wheel and a boat of air and steel
To float upon the Queen's highway!
Oh give me the kiss of the morning breeze,
And the rose of the morning sky,
And the long brown road where the tired spirit's load
Slips off as the leagues go by.

T. W. ROLLESTON.

THE INVASION OF BRITTANY

In fair Queen Paris, beneath the trees,
'Mid a blaze of cafés, a throng of men,
Whose speech tossed up on the warm night breeze
Is scattered like spray ere it rise again,
I have loitered forgotten and yet been fain
Of the Queen of the world and her sorceries,
But to-day she has filled up her cup in vain,
For our way to the Breton seaboard lies.

In old German woodlands, many a day,
I have lost myself to lie at peace,
'Mid the trooping pines, where the children play,
Till the light grows faint and the shadows increase,
And the cloud-drift hangs in a rose-bloom fleece
Where the dim blue Saxon highlands rise,
But, cease from thy spells, O Elbeland, cease,
For our way to the Breton seaboard lies.

In waking dreams I have travelled far
By swamps where the yellow reeds grow free,
Where India sits on a jewelled car
Or the spice-winds blow over Araby;
Chrysanthemum country were fair to see
And dainty its maids with the almond eyes,
But dreams must fade when the stars decree,
And our way to the Breton seaboard lies.

In the narrow streets of the grey old town
The gables tower to meet the skies,
And the windworn bastions grimly frown
On the strand where the Breton seaboard lies.

ARTHUR CECIL HILLIER.

TO A BRETON BEGGAR

(Dol Cathedral)

In the brown shadow of the transept door,
  Grey kings and granite prophets overhead,
Which are so ancient they can age no more,
  A beggar begs his bread.

He too is old,—so old, and worn, and still,
  He seems a part of those gaunt sculptures there,
By wizard masons dowered with power and will
  To moan sometimes in prayer:—

To moan in prayer, moving thin carven lips,
  And with faint senses striving to drink in
Some golden sound which peradventure slips
  From the altar's heart within.

What is thy prayer? Is it a plaintive praise,
  An intercession, or an anguished plaint;
Remorse, O sinner, for wild vanished days,
  Or ecstasy, O saint?

And through long hours, when thou art wont to sit
  In moveless silence, what inspires thy thought?
Is thine an utter drowsing; or shall wit
  Still travail, memory-fraught?

Hear'st thou old battles? Wast thou one of those
  Whose angry fire-locks made the hillsides ring,
When, clad in skins and rags, the Chouans rose
  To die for Church and King?

Or dost thou view, in weird and sad array,
  The long-dead Cymry—they of whom men tell
That always to the war they marched away,
  And that they always fell?

So moving are thine eyes which cannot see,
  So great a resignation haunts thy face,
I often think that I behold in thee
  The symbol of thy race:

Not as it was when bards Armorican
  Sang the high pageant of their Age of Gold;
But as it is, a sombre long-tressed man,
  Exceeding poor and old,

With somewhat in his eyes for some to read,
  Albeit dimmed with years and scarcely felt,—
The mystery of an antique deathless Creed,
  The glamour of the Celt.

VICTOR PLARR.

GLORIES

Roses from Paestan rosaries!
More goodly red and white was she:
Her red and white were harmonies,
Not matched upon a Paestan tree.

Ivories blaunched in Alban air!
She lies more purely blaunched than you:
No Alban whiteness doth she wear,
But death's perfection of that hue.

Nay! now the rivalry is done,
Of red, and white, and whiter still:
She hath a glory from that sun,
Who falls not from Olympus hill.

Lionel Johnson.

THE SONG OF TRISTRAM

THE star of love is trembling in the west,
  Night hears the desolate sea with moan on moan
  Sigh for the storm, who on his mountains lone
Smites his wild harp and dreams of her wild breast.
        I am thy storm, Isolt, and thou my sea!
                Isolt!
        My passionate sea!

The storm to her wild breast, the passionate sea
  To his fierce arms: we to the rapturous leap
  Of mated spirits mingling in love's deep,
Flame to flame, I to thee and thou to me!
        Thou to mine arms, Isolt, I to thy breast!
                Isolt!
        I to thy breast!

JOHN TODHUNTER.

TO ONE IN BEDLAM

WITH delicate, mad hands, behind his sordid bars,
Surely he hath his posies, which they tear and twine ;
Those scentless wisps of straw, that miserably line
His strait, caged universe, whereat the dull world stares,

Pedant and pitiful. O, how his rapt gaze wars
With their stupidity! Know they what dreams divine
Lift his long, laughing reveries like enchanted wine,
And make his melancholy germane to the stars' ?

O lamentable brother ! if those pity thee,
Am I not fain of all thy lone eyes promise me;
Half a fool's kingdom, far from men who sow and reap,
All their days, vanity ? Better than mortal flowers,
Thy moon-kissed roses seem : better than love or sleep,
The star-crowned solitude of thine oblivious hours!

ERNEST DOWSON.

PROSERPINE

(For a Picture)

RULER of Darkness, Queen of desolate Night,
Thee whom the innumerable Dead salute
With myriad-murmuring homage, thee the fruit
Red-riven dooms to banishment from light.

Farewell, Sicilian orchards flowerful-bright!
Farewell, the smiling of the sun! no lute
Of Orpheus shall revoke thee from the mute
Sad shadow-realm where thou art lapped in night.

Thee those far voices that thy name repeat,
Charm not, with bent ear listening; nor thine eyes,
Wild like a fawn's, seek Enna's flowers and wheat;

For thou hast found more fair the sunless skies,
More blest the royalty of Death, more sweet
His love whose lone domain in darkness lies.

G. A. GREENE.

THE FOLK OF THE AIR

O'Driscoll drove with a song
  The wild duck and the drake
From the tall and the tufted reeds
  Of the drear Heart Lake.

And he saw how the reeds grew dark
  At the coming of night tide,
And dreamed of the long dim hair
  Of Bridget his bride.

He heard while he sang and dreamed
  A piper piping away,
And never was piping so sad,
  And never was piping so gay.

And he saw young men and young girls
  Who danced on a level place,
And Bridget his bride among them,
  With a sad and a gay face.

The dancers crowded about him,
And many a sweet thing said,
And a young man brought him red wine,
And a young girl white bread.

But Bridget drew him by the sleeve,
Away from the merry bands,
To old men playing at cards
With a twinkling of ancient hands.

The bread and the wine had a doom,
For these were the folk of the air;
He sat and played in a dream
Of her long dim hair.

He played with the merry old men,
And thought not of evil chance,
Until one bore Bridget his bride
Away from the merry dance.

He bore her away in his arms,
The handsomest young man there,
And his neck and his breast and his arms
Were drowned in her long dim hair.

O'Driscoll got up from the grass
  And scattered the cards with a cry;
But the old men and dancers were gone
  As a cloud faded into the sky.

He knew now the folk of the air,
  And his heart was blackened by dread,
And he ran to the door of his house;
  Old women were keening the dead;

But he heard high up in the air
  A piper piping away;
And never was piping so sad,
  And never was piping so gay.

W. B. YEATS.

SONG

OH what know they of harbours
Who toss not on the sea !
They tell of fairer havens,
But none so fair there be

As Plymouth town outstretching
Her quiet arms to me,
Her breast's broad welcome spreading
From Mewstone to Penlee.

Ah with this home-thought, darling,
Come crowding thoughts of thee—
Oh, what know they of harbours
Who toss not on the sea !

ERNEST RADFORD.

LOVE'S EXCHANGE

SIMPLE am I, I care no whit
For pelf or place,
It is enough for me to sit
And watch Dulcinea's face;
To mark the lights and shadows flit
Across the silver moon of it.

I have no other merchandise,
No stocks or shares,
No other gold but just what lies
In those deep eyes of hers ;
And, sure, if all the world were wise,
It too would bank within her eyes.

I buy up all her smiles all day,
With all my love,
And sell them back, cost price, or, say,
A kiss or two above;
It is a speculation fine,
The profit must be always mine.

The world has many things, 'tis true,
  To fill its time,
Far more important things to do
  Than making love and rhyme;
Yet, if it asked me to advise,
I'd say buy up Dulcinea's eyes !

RICHARD LE GALLIENNE.

IN EXCELSIS

Above the world at our window seat
All the murmur of London rises high,
From the hansoms racing along the street,
And the flaring stalls and the passers-by.

As the lamps of a rolling carriage gleam
You may catch for a moment a woman's face,
And a soft-robed figure—a vanishing dream
Of a white burnoose and a flutter of lace.

One argent star o'er the clock-tower wakes
More pure than the spark of a Northern night,
Where the sleeping woodlands and lonely lakes
Wed the splendour of frost to the glory of light.

Above the world at our window-sill
O'er the countless roofs of the city of care,
The darkness falls, and my pulses thrill
At the touch of thy cheek and the scent of thine hair.

We have lived here long through the dreary days
Of the sun and the rain and the trodden snow:
We have watched of an evening the heaven ablaze
With the smoky glare of the afterglow.

We have lived together and known great joys
And have sorrowed for much beyond recall,
And been soiled with the dust and deafened with noise,
And the crowd heeds not, but the stars know all.

ARTHUR CECIL HILLIER.

LOVE AND ART

The sun went indistinguishably down
  Over the murky town,
Night droops about the houses heavily;
  The Temple gateways gape and frown,
But, as I enter, strangely, comes to me
The odour of patchouli.

Ah, there she flits before me, whose gay scent
  Betrays the way she went;
A corner intercepts her, she is gone;
  And as I follow, indolent,
My visiting mind, with her to muse upon,
Runs curiously on.

I seem to hear her mount the narrow stair,
  Creaking, for all her care,
And now a door flies open, just above,
  And now she laughs, to see him there,
His arms about her, and both babble of
The nonsense-verse of love.

I enter and forget them, for to-night
  I have my verse to write,
That love-song, I have yet to pare and trim.
  So, should it be ? or—God ! the light
In that revealing casement-square grows dim :
He kisses her, and I but write of him !

ARTHUR SYMONS.

A YEAR OF THE RIVER

THE Spring is here, the Spring is free
From bonds of Winter's jealousy,
The river is alive to-day:
She puts on blue, and puts off grey:
She laughs, and dances, and puts on
The daisies, and the dazzling swan,
The leaping moon along her waves,
And merrier foam that bounds and raves.

And now she rolls the buds, and now
The buds are leaves; the willows bow.
The chestnuts fling their white; the May
Comes hastening in the same glad day,
Till mightier strength of Summer's hand
Opens new heavens above our land,
And all the gifts the world has known
Return, like birds a moment flown.

I shared the day with every bird,
And what the kingfisher has heard
I heard, and saw in Summer noon
The little splash, the ripple's moon.
And evening with her golden space
That makes the swallow's darting place
Has widened out her peace for me
And watched her children silently.

Then call me not away while yet
No frost, nor storms, nor mists have met
Nor sorrow paints the world in grey,
Nor labour lives at war with day,
Or night is dark as sepulture,
While rattling trees affright the shore
With semblances of deathly bones,
And wind bewails in undertones.

For, even then, in lighted rooms
I feel at heart the unheeded glooms
Where—through a humble moon and pale
Wanders along the windy vale
And labours with the heavy stress
Of cloudy motion limitless,
Like sorrow where I feel no part,
And yet that whispers near my heart.

Oh come but once, come out alone
And see what secret thing is known
In silence of the winter stream.
She needs no pity in her dream;
She only wears the face of grief
As Summer with the golden sheaf
Puts on the mask of joy awhile
And bids our easy hours to smile.

But here the shadow owns an art
That teaches each o'er-tired heart
A skill unknown to noisy Spring,
Unknown to Summer on the wing,
Unknown to Autumn satisfied,
The art to see, and stand aside;
To look on grief as only grief,
And death as but a fallen leaf.

Here Spring, impatient of her tears,
Here Summer, wrath in weeping years
And flinging thunder upon rain,
Here Autumn numbering her grain,
And busy in her golden stores,
While hour by hour the sorrow pours
That grieves the fading of the year,
All these are dumb and foolish here.

But wintry night and solitude
That lean upon the stream to brood
Hold silence deep to float the word
Across the inspired spaces heard
Between the stars, beyond the gloom
Of years that in the eternal womb
Are not as yet brought forth for tears:
Then we make peace with our brief years.

I hear her as the midnight weeps,
I hear her as the echo sleeps
Forgetting what the Spring bird knows,
I hear her as the quiet flows;
And who shall come with me to roam
Along her shore, shall turn to home
And bring a quiet thing like this,
The patient River will not miss.

EDWIN J. ELLIS.

NOON-DAY

Elegiacs

WIND, O wind of the Spring, thine old enchantment renewing,
  How at the shock of thy might wakens a cry within me!
Out of what wonderful lands never trodden by man, never told of,
  Lands where never a ship anchored or trafficker fared,
Comest thou, breathing like flame till the brown earth flames into blossom,
  Quickening the sap of old woods swayed in thy stormy embrace,
Rousing in depths of the heart the wild waves of an infinite longing,
  Longing for freedom and life, longing for Springs that are dead?

Surely the far blue sea, foam-flecked with the speed of
thy coming,
Brightened in laughter abroad, sang at the feet of
the isles,
Stirred in a tumult of joy, as my soul stirs trembling
with passion,
Trembling with passion and hope, wild with the
spirit of Spring.
Ah, what dreams rearise, half pain half bliss to re-
member,
Hearing the storm of thy song, blown from the
height of the skies :
Something remains upon earth to be done, to be dared,
to be sought for.
Up with the anchor again! out with the sails to the
blast!
Out to the shock of the seas that encircle the Fortunate
Islands,
Vision and promise and prize, home of the Wind of
the Spring!

T. W. ROLLESTON.

SONG OF THE WULFSHAW LARCHES

HEART of Earth, let us be gone,
From this rock where we have stayed
While the sun has risen and shone
Ten thousand times, and thrown our shade
Always in the self-same place.

Now the night draws on apace:
The day is dying on the height,
The wind brings cold sea-fragrance here,
And cries, and restless murmurings,
Now night is near,—
Of wings and feet that take to flight,
Of furry feet and feathery wings
That take their joyous flight at will
Away and over the hiding hill,
And into the land where the sun has fled.

O let us go, as they have sped,—
The soft swift shapes that left us here,
The gentle things that came and went
And left us in imprisonment!
Let us be gone, as they have gone,
Away, and into the hidden lands;—
From rock and turf our roots uptear,
Break from the clinging keeping bands,
Out of this long imprisoning break;
At last, our sunward journey take,
And far, to-night, and farther on,—
Heart of Earth, let us be gone!

ERNEST RHYS.

TO MORFYDD

A VOICE on the winds,
A voice by the waters,
  Wanders and cries:

Oh! what are the winds?
And what are the waters?
  Mine are your eyes.

Western the winds are,
And western the waters,
  Where the light lies:

Oh! what are the winds?
And what are the waters?
  Mine are your eyes!

Cold, cold, grow the winds,
And dark grow the waters,
  Where the sun dies:

Oh! what are the winds?
And what are the waters?
Mine are your eyes!

And down the night winds,
And down the night waters,
The music flies:

Oh! what are the winds?
And what are the waters?
Cold be the winds,
And wild be the waters,
So mine be your eyes!

LIONEL JOHNSON.

DEER IN GREENWICH PARK

Pathetic in their rags, from far and near,
The children of the slum o'er-swarm the grass :
Pathetic in their grace, the Greenwich deer
Leap up to let them pass.

Where riot scares the gloom, and fevers burn,
These wizened babes were pent till morning light :
Slim shadows moving 'mong the moonlit fern
The shy deer strayed all night.

In the hot hours London's poor wastrels find
Their paradise in this brown London park :
The lordlier brutes, in the scant shade reclin'd,
Pant for the hours of dark,

When some dim instinct from primæval years
Thrills, on a sudden, through each dappled breast,
And with untameable mysterious fears
The herd is re-possessed !

Then the branch'd horns are tossed; the nostrils fine
  Respire the sleepy breath from London's heart,
And bucks, and does, and fawns, in spectral line,
  Forth from their bracken start.

An antlered watchman stamps a shapely hoof:
  —Is that a tartan'd Gael within the brake?
Did Luath bay below the heath-clad roof—
  Doth Fingal's son awake?

Hath a harp wailed in Tara? Did a bough
  Snap in Broceliande, where Merlin keeps
His drowsy magic vigil even now
  In the oakwood's sunlit deeps?

Was it a cry borne from Caerluda town,—
  A spell the Stag of Ages understands?
Or voices of old rivers raving down
  Through many heathery lands?

Or—since the red stag by wild mountain streams
  Is he whom such weird terrors most appal;
Since these are fallow deer, and yonder dreams
  The dom'd Stuart Hospital,—

Was it the bugle echoing as of yore
  In some vast chase, enwrapt in lake-side mists?
Swept Herne the Hunter by, or score on score
  Of silken Royalists?

Hunts captured Charles? or hath Cromwellian shot
  Laid some escaping war-spent gallant low
In the far ride, where last year's leaf doth rot,
  And, save the deer, none go?

Who knows what stirs them? Nay, can any guess
  That which their beautiful clear eyes import
When, at high noon, about your hand they press,
  Begging in timid sort,

Save haply the exile's doom, which is the same
  Whether 'tis buried in the tragic eyes
Of king discrowned, or wanderer without name,
  Bondman, or brute that dies?

VICTOR PLARR.

NON SUM QUALIS ERAM BONAE SUB REGNO CYNARAE

Last night, ah, yesternight, betwixt her lips and mine
There fell thy shadow, Cynara ! thy breath was shed
Upon my soul, between the kisses and the wine;
And I was desolate and sick of an old passion,
  Yea ! I grew desolate and bowed my head;
I have been faithful to thee, Cynara ! in my fashion.

All night upon my breast I felt her warm heart beat;
Night-long within mine arms in love and sleep she lay:
Surely the kisses of her bought, red mouth were sweet ?
But I was desolate and sick of an old passion,
  When I awoke, and found the dawn was grey:
I have been faithful to thee, Cynara ! in my fashion.

I have forgot much, Cynara ! gone with the wind;
Flung roses, roses riotously with the throng;
Dancing to put thy pale, lost lilies out of mind;
But I was desolate, and sick of an old passion,
  Yea ! all the time because the dance was long !
I have been faithful to thee, Cynara ! in my fashion.

I cried for madder music, and for stronger wine;
But when the feast is finished, and the lamps expire,
Then falls thy shadow, Cynara! the night is thine;
And I am desolate and sick of an old passion,
  Yea! hungry for the lips of my desire:—
I have been faithful to thee, Cynara! in my fashion!

ERNEST DOWSON.

EUTHANASIA

(*Fin de siècle*)

YES, this rich death were best :
Lay poison on thy lips, kiss me to sleep,
Or on the siren billow of thy breast
Bring some voluptuous Lethe for life's pain,
Some languorous nepenthe that will creep
Drowsily from vein to vein;
That slowly, drowsily, will steep
Sense after sense, till, down long gulfs of rest
Whirled like a leaf, I sink to the lone deep.

It shall be afternoon,
And roses, roses breathing in the air !
Deliciously the splendour of deep June,
Tempered through amber draperies, round us fall;
And, like a dream of Titian, let thy hair
Bosom and arms glow all,
Clouds of love's sunset, o'er me there :
Kiss that last kiss; then low some golden tune
Sing, for the dirge of our superb despair.

So let the clock tick on,
Measuring the soft pulsations of Time's wing,
While to the pulseless ocean, like a swan
Abandoned to an unrelenting stream,
Floating, I hear thee faint and fainter sing;
Till death athwart my dream
Shall glide, robed like a Magian king,
And ease with poppies of oblivion
This heart, the scorpion Life no more may sting.

JOHN TODHUNTER.

VIOLETS full, and the wild birds' song,
Where the leaves grow green;
Where wind-flowers blow, and the blackbirds throng
In their haunts unseen;
Where the primroses peep,
Here let me lie,
Let me lie,
Till I drink, in my sleep,
A memory of flowers
From the unforgotten hours,
And the perfume of the days gone by.

Violets closed, and the wild birds hushed,
Where the dead leaves fall!
O the days when our sunrise flushed
Red rays over all!

Where the brown owls peep,
Here let me lie,
Let me lie,
Where the years fell asleep,
Let me mourn for the flowers
Of the unforgotten hours,
And the perfume of the days gone by.

G. A. GREENE.

THE SECOND CRUCIFIXION

Loud mockers in the roaring street
  Say Christ is crucified again,
Twice pierced His Gospel-bringing feet,
  Twice broken His great heart in vain.

I hear, and to myself I smile,
For Christ talks with me all the while.

No angel now to roll the stone
  From off His unawaking sleep,
In vain shall Mary watch alone,
  In vain the soldiers vigil keep.

Yet, while they deem my Lord is dead,
My eyes are on His shining head.

Ah! never more shall Mary hear
  That voice exceeding sweet and low
Within the garden calling clear,
  Her Lord is gone, and she must go.

Yet all the while my Lord I meet
In every London lane and street.

Poor Lazarus shall wait in vain,
  And Bartimæus still go blind;
The healing hem shall ne'er again
  Be touched by suffering humankind.

Yet all the while I see them rest,
The poor and outcast, in His breast.

No more unto the stubborn heart
  With gentle knocking shall He plead,
No more the mystic pity start,
  For Christ twice dead is dead indeed.

So in the street I hear men say,
Yet Christ is with me all the day.

RICHARD LE GALLIENNE.

THE FIDDLER OF DOONEY

When I play on my fiddle in Dooney,
  Folk dance like a wave of the sea.
My brother is priest in Kilvarnet,
  My cousin in Rossnaree.

I passed my brother and cousin,
  They read in a book of prayer;
I read in a book of songs
  I bought at the Sligo Fair.

When we come, at the close of Time,
  To Peter sitting in state,
He will smile on the three old spirits,
  But call me first through the gate.

For the good are always the merry,
  Save by an evil chance,
And the merry love the fiddle,
  And the merry love to dance.

And when the folk there spy me,
  They will all come up to me,
With 'Here is the fiddler of Dooney!'
  And dance like a wave of the sea.

W. B. YEATS.

ORPHEUS IN COVENT GARDEN

Down from the cliffs that rise sheer out of hell
He gazed awhile as one that masters doubt:
Then o'er the dark ravine the golden spell
Of clear-struck lyre and thrilling voice rang out.

As oft amid the Thracian hills of yore
The pard grew tame and fawned about his feet,
So they that wandered by that dolorous shore
Hung tranced upon that voice divinely sweet.

Around the charmer in the Indian land
The snakes cease not to sway their cunning heads,
And flap their dusky coils upon the sand
The while his reed a sleepy music sheds.

So that clear harp that clashed through all its strings
Soothed those within the gate of triple brass,
Until they mused upon forgotten things
Seen faintly as the shadows in a glass.

For us once more the antique lyre is strung
That gave the lost Eurydice release,
Since one whose birthright is the perfect tongue
Of Italy brings back the art of Greece.

ARTHUR CECIL HILLIER.

SONG IN THE LABOUR MOVEMENT

THE voice of labour soundeth shrill,
  Mere clamour of a tuneless throng,
To you who barter at your will
  The very life that maketh song.

Oh, you whose sluggard hours are spent
  The rule of Mammon to prolong,
What know you of the stern intent
  Of hosted labour marching strong?

When we have righted what is wrong
  Great singing shall your ears entreat;
Meanwhile in movement there is song,
  And music in the pulse of feet.

ERNEST RADFORD.

EVENING

(*Evensong*)

In the heart of a Saxon forest I followed the winding
ways
Deep cushioned with moss and barred with the sunset's slanting rays.

When out of the distance dim, where no end to the
path was seen,
But the breath of the Springtime hung like a motion-
less mist of green,

I heard a sound of singing, unearthly sad and clear,
Rise from the forest deeps and float on the evening
air.

I stopped and wondered and waited as it nearer and
nearer grew,
Louder and still more loud, till at last came into view—

No vision of spirits told of in weird old forest lore
Who roam the greenwood singing for ever and evermore—

But six Teutonic maidens tanned with the rain and
sun,
A burthen of billetted wood on the shoulders of every
one.

How sturdily by they marched! and the chanting
passed away
In the fragrant depths of the forest, and died with the
dying day.

No spirits indeed—yet I thought, as awhile in dreams
I stood,
That a music more than earthly had passed through
the darkening wood.

And I thought that the day to the morrow bequeathed
in that solemn strain
The whole world's hope and labour, its love and its
ancient pain.

T. W. Rolleston.

PEACE

Poor Peace, long silent in the market-place
  Stood sadly like a slave, where none would buy her;
Yet now and then, there moved upon her face
  A mother's smile whose children tire and try her,
And now and then she looked within her veil
That bound her breast and throat and forehead pale.

But while she bent within the silent folding
  Where looped and swayed the veil beneath her breast,
It seemed some secret she was given for holding,
  Some secret like a little child at rest,
And now with less of patient grief she smiled;
She had much solace from the sleeping child.

The market roared and rang all day around her:
  The buyer told his ever-new contempt,
The seller praised himself, but no one found her—
  From all the discord and the strife exempt,
Till night came softly, and the moon rose pale,
The mad world slept, and Peace unbound her veil.

And then, as when deep organ-music rolls
  One sound is lifted on a thousand prayers,
The child came forth, one form, a thousand souls,
  And now, from house to house, up quiet stairs
The gentle feet of his meek nurse neglected
Bore him, by men's oblivion less rejected.

And stepping softly to each fool forgetful
  Peace gave them back their souls for silent keeping;
But some she saw, and turned away, regretful,
  She could not trust their souls to them in sleeping,
And some, the teller of the old tale said,
She will but partly trust when they are dead.

EDWIN J. ELLIS.

SONG

WHAT are lips, but to be kissed?
  What are eyes, but to be praised?
What the fineness of a wrist?
  What the slimness of a waist?
What the softness of her hair,
If not that Love be tangled there?

What are lips, not to be kissed?
  What are eyes, not to be praised?
What is she, that would resist
  Love's desire to be embraced?
What her heart that will not dare
Suffer poor Love to linger there?

These are lips, fond to be kissed,
  These are eyes, fain to be praised:
And I think, if Love has missed
  Shelter in the wintry waste,
That this heart may soon prepare
Some nook for him to nestle there.

ARTHUR SYMONS.

DEATH AND THE PLAYER

I WATCHED the players playing on their stage;
An old delightful comedy was theirs,
The very picture of a gallant age,
Full of majestic airs.

Wit, virtuoso, captain, stately lord,—
Each played his part with smooth Augustan grace,
And, grey and curled, th' Olympian perruques soared
O'er each fine oval face.

Anon, young Celia, poised on high red heels,
Advanced with Chloe, the discreet soubrette:
Her laughter rings abroad in silver peals;
Her courtiers fawn and fret.

One was a whiskered son of awful Mars;
And one, the favourite, a thing of spleen,
Whose pasquil jests, a stream of falling stars,
Illumined all the scene.

They trod a minuet, and evermore,
  Betwixt the curtseying lady and her thrall,
A masked and shrouded dancer kept the floor,
    Unnoted by them all.

Alas, poor player, that was Death's Dance indeed!
  The curtain fell; the masker's fleshless hand
Compelled thee to his chariot, which with speed
    Rolled home to his own land.

And now with cheeks and eyelids that confess
  Grim stains of the last midnight's gay disguise,
Th' ingenious haggard actors swiftly press
    Where their dead brother lies.

How strange a graveside—oh, how strange a scene!
  The player's double life in such eclipse!
What a morality would this have been
    On those once mocking lips!

But they are dumb, and there's scarce time for tears.
  Back to the town! They're clamouring for our plays.
'Tis good that arch-comedian Death appears
    But once in many days!

VICTOR PLARR.

IN OPERA-LAND

WHERE almond blossoms shed their snow
From garden walls of grey old Spain,
The Tritons of the fountain blow
Columns that break in diamond rain;
And 'neath the stars Elvira's voice
Bewails her fate in accents bland
Unto the gallant of her choice,
As is the mode in Opera-land.

Zerlina loosens her dark hair
And sings a snatch before the glass,
And brigands flirt with ladies fair
Who yield unto their charms, alas!
Their lords have pockets stuffed with gold
And boast their treasure to the band;
We know that way they have of old,
For it is mode in Opera-land.

In this last refuge of romance
Crusaders yet may hold their own,
And wandering gipsy girls may dance
Where camps are pitched and trumpets blown,
And soldiers dice upon the drums,
And pennons on the tents are fanned
By every wayward breeze that comes,
Such breeze as blows through Opera-land.

Assassins enter tightly masked,
And peasants trip it on the sod,
And guests arrive at balls unasked,
And statues in the churchyard nod,
And heroines march on serene
Through corpses strewn on either hand,
Nor ever show surprise, I ween;
It is not mode in Opera-land.

When these are laid upon the shelf,
Some Ibsenitish lady free
Her duty to her sex and self
May vaunt upon the natural B:
When moonlight and romance are dimmed
And old-world shrines no longer stand,
Ye gods! what will be preached and hymned
Within the realms of Opera-land!

Bold gipsy girls whose love is light,
And hermits of the desert sand,
Long be it ere your charms are trite
And ways are changed in Opera-land.

ARTHUR CECIL HILLIER.

GROWTH

I WATCHED the glory of her childhood change,
Half-sorrowful to find the child I knew,
  (Loved long ago in lily-time)
Become a maid, mysterious and strange,
With fair, pure eyes—dear eyes, but not the eyes I knew
    Of old, in the olden time!

Till on my doubting soul the ancient good
Of her dear childhood in the new disguise
  Dawned, and I hastened to adore
The glory of her waking maidenhood,
And found the old tenderness within her deepening eyes,
    But kinder than before.

ERNEST DOWSON.

QUATRAINS

Conscience (the Obverse)

CONSCIENCE is that fine critic of each thrill
  Along the spirit's nerves, with instinct sane
  For life's fine art assaying joy and pain,
His loves and hates canons of good and ill.

Conscience (the Reverse)

Conscience is but a child who fears the rod
Laid on by Mrs Grundy or by God ;
  But whose the stroke, or why they smite or sparc
The smarting child scarce guesses. That is odd !

JOHN TODHUNTER.

The Arch Magician

Art thou a man? Within thy mind's high hall
A magic mirror hangs upon the wall
From out whose crystal dim the Magian, Thought,
Summons the shapes that ravish and appal.

JOHN TODHUNTER.

The New Sinai

Women were poets once, and dumbly wrought
Sweet love-songs from the perilous stuff of Thought,
Now they have learnt to speak in dreadful prose,
Thundering in our dazed ears their *must* and *ought*.

JOHN TODHUNTER.

Creation

Behind me lay life's endless avatars,
  Before me vague unfathomable dread,
  In wastes of space where Death himself was dead :
Then God went by me, silent, sowing stars.

JOHN TODHUNTER.

The Golden Key

To love the right things rightly : this enspheres
  Wisdom, religion, art ; forges the key
That opens Eden through the Gate of Tears,
  Where by life's river blooms the mystic Tree.

JOHN TODHUNTER.

THE DARK ANGEL

Dark Angel, with thine aching lust
To rid the world of penitence:
Malicious Angel, who still dost
My soul such subtile violence!

Because of thee, no thought, no thing,
Abides for me undesecrate:
Dark Angel, ever on the wing,
Who never reachest me too late!

When music sounds, then changest thou
Its silvery to a sultry fire:
Nor will thine envious heart allow
Delight untortured by desire.

Through thee, the gracious Muses turn
To Furies, O mine Enemy!
And all the things of beauty burn
With flames of evil ecstasy.

Because of thee, the land of dreams
Becomes a gathering place of fears;
Until tormented slumber seems
One vehemence of useless tears.

When sunlight glows upon the flowers,
Or ripples down the dancing sea:
Thou, with thy troop of passionate powers,
Beleaguerest, bewilderest me.

Within the breath of autumn woods,
Within the winter silences:
Thy venomous spirit stirs and broods,
O master of impieties!

The ardour of red flame is thine,
And thine the steely soul of ice:
Thou poisonest the fair design
Of nature, with unfair device.

Apples of ashes, golden bright;
Waters of bitterness, how sweet:
O banquet of a foul delight,
Prepared by thee, dark Paraclete!

Thou art the whisper in the gloom,
The hinting tone, the haunting laugh:
Thou art the adorner of my tomb,
The minstrel of mine epitaph.

I fight thee, in the Holy Name!
Yet, what thou dost, is what God saith:
Tempter! should I escape thy flame,
Thou wilt have helped my soul from death:

The second death, that never dies,
That cannot die, when time is dead:
Live death, wherefrom the lost soul cries,
Eternally uncomforted.

Dark Angel, with thine aching lust!
Of two defeats, of two despairs:
Less dread, a change to drifting dust,
Than thine eternity of cares.

Do what thou wilt, thou shalt not so,
Dark Angel! triumph over me:
Lonely, *unto the Lone I go;*
Divine, *to the Divinity.*

LIONEL JOHNSON.

A MOOD

'*They have taken away my Lord, and I know not where they have laid him.*'

THEY have taken away my Lord;
They have shattered the one great Hope;
They have left us alone to cope
With our terrible selves: the sword

They broke, which the world restored;
They have cast down the King from on high;
Their derision has scaled the sky;
They have taken away my Lord.

The strength of immortal Love;
The comfort of millions that weep;
Prayer, and the Cross we adored—
All is lost! there is no one above:
We are left like the beasts that creep:
They have taken away our Lord.

G. A. GREENE.

A MYSTICAL PRAYER TO THE MASTERS OF THE ELEMENTS, FINVARRA, FEACRA, AND CAOLTE

THE Powers, not kind like you, came where God's
 garden blows,
 And stole the crimson Rose,
And hurled it from its place amid the pearly light
 Into the blinding night,—
O, when shall Sorrow wander no more in the land
 With Beauty hand in hand?

Great elemental Powers of wind, and wave, and fire,
 With your harmonious quire,
Encircle her I love and sing her into peace,
 That my old care may cease,
And she forget the wandering and the crimson gloom
 Of the Rose in its doom.

Great Rulers of stillness, let her no longer be
As the light on the sea,
Or as the changing spears flung by the golden stars
Out of their whirling cars,
But let a gentle silence enwrought with music flow
Where her soft footsteps go.

W. B. Yeats.

HESPERIDES

Men say—beyond the Western seas
  The happy isles no longer glow,
No sailor sights Hesperides,
  All that was long ago.

No longer in a glittering morn
  Their misty meadows flicker nigh,
No singing with the spray is borne,
  All that is long gone by.

To-day upon the golden beach
  No gold-haired guardian maidens stand,
No apples ripen out of reach,
  And none are mad to land.

The merchant-men, 'tis they say so,
  That trade across the Western seas,
In hurried transit to and fro,
  About Hesperides.

But, Reader, not as these thou art,
  So loose thy shallop from its hold,
And, trusting to the ancient chart,
  Thou'lt make them as of old.

RICHARD LE GALLIENNE.

ACKNOWLEDGMENT

Addressed to H.E.T.

FAIR flowers! the hand I fain would kiss
That so among you lightly moved,
To gather this—and this—and this—
The—while you nodded and approved.

In culling leaves so rare of scent,
It was—was it not—her intent
To grace a friendship old as ours
With fragrance passing that of flowers?

ERNEST RADFORD.

NIGHT

(After all)

WHEN the time comes for me to die,
  To-morrow, or some other day,
If God should bid me make reply,
  'What would'st thou ?' I shall say,

O God, Thy world was great and fair;
  Yet give me to forget it clean !
Vex me no more with things that were,
  And things that might have been.

I loved, I toiled, throve ill or well,
  —Lived certain years and murmured not.
Now grant me in that land to dwell
  Where all things are forgot.

For others, Lord, Thy purging fires,
  The loves reknit, the crown, the palm.
For me, the death of all desires
  In deep, eternal calm.

T. W. ROLLESTON.

SAINT ANTHONY

ALAS, poor Saint, you saw her too—
  The white white bird, our spirits' lure.
Ah, then at last, at first you knew
  How fair is fair, how pure is pure.
Why did she tempt your heaven-bound sense?
What devil had she?
Her innocence.

And when you turned with laughter loud,
  Though inward filled with hurrying fears,
Because your promised life was proud,
  Nor might she know your fount of tears,
What angel moved with reverence
Your secret prayer?
Her innocence.

EDWIN J. ELLIS.

TO O. E.

Olwen, all the harps are still,
That would once have chimed for you
From the haunted fields of Wales!
Buried deep in Merlin's Hill,
Lost the lyric note they knew;
Now no more their bardic thrill
Stirs our pulses through and through:
And our later music fails.

Ernest Rhys.

A VARIATION UPON LOVE

For God's sake let me love you, and give over
These tedious protestations of a lover;
We're of one mind to love, and there's no let:
Remember that, and all the rest forget.
And let's be happy, mistress, while we may,
Ere yet to-morrow shall be called to-day.
To-morrow may be heedless, idle-hearted:
One night's enough for love to have met and parted.
Then be it now, and I'll not say that I
In many several deaths for you would die;
And I'll not ask you to declare that you
Will longer love than women mostly do.
Leave words to them whom words, not doings, move,
And let our silence answer for our love.

Arthur Symons.

A SECRET OF THE SEA

Down at the bottom of the sea,
  The huge old galleon lies asleep;
Red seaweeds cloak her heavily,
  Green seaweeds round her droop and sweep.

Scarce any light descends to show
  Her decks made black with ancient blood,
Or the few bones that dimly glow
  Where her stout captain last withstood

The drunken shock of his wild crew,
  Who welcomed freedom in his fall
With laughter, cursing, tears, and who
  Met with such shipwreck after all!

'Tis years since the faint noontide beam,
  That filters to the chart-room floor,
Last rested where, as in a dream,
  The drowned chief mutineer would pore

With orbits void and bony hands
  Upon the chart, which, day by day,
Into new shapes of seas and lands
  The exploring sea-worms fret and fray—

Years since that semblance of a man,
  That relic of unknown despair,
That symbol of past crime, began
  Obscurely to be no more there!

For centuries now the ship hath lain
  Down at the bottom of the sea,
Unknown, alone, save for some train
  Of shy small fishes starting by,

And so she still must lie until
  A dying sun be burning red,
And earthquakes all earth's caverns thrill,
  And the deep sea give up its dead!

VICTOR PLARR.

IN AN OLD LIBRARY

Here the still air
Broods over drowsy nooks
Of ancient learning: one is ware,
As in a mystic aisle
Of lingering incense, of the balm of books.
So nard from cerecloths of Egyptian kings
Solemnised once the sepulchres of Nile.

Here quietness,
A ghostly presence, dwells
Among rich tombs; here doth possess
With an ecstatic dread
The intruder seeking old-world oracles
In books, centuries of books, centuries of tombs
That hold the spirits of the crownèd dead.

Go softly! Here
Sleep fair embalmèd souls
In piled-up monuments, in their sere

And blazoned robes of fame,
Conquerors of Time. Whisper to these grey scrolls,
Call Poet, Sage, Romancer, Chronicler,
And every one will answer to his name.

Man walks the earth,
The quintessence of dust:
Books from the ashes of his mirth,
Madness, and sorrow, seem
To draw the elixir of some rarer gust,
Or, like the stone of Alchemy, transmute
Life's cheating dross to golden truth of dream.

JOHN TODHUNTER.

THE GARDEN OF SHADOW

Love heeds no more the sighing of the wind
Against the perfect flowers: thy garden's close
Is grown a wilderness, where none shall find
One strayed, last petal of one last year's rose.

O bright, bright hair! O mouth like a ripe fruit!
Can famine be so nigh to harvesting?
Love that was songful, with a broken lute
In grass of graveyards goeth murmuring.

Let the wind blow against the perfect flowers,
And all thy garden change and glow with spring:
Love is grown blind; with no more count of hours,
Nor part in seed-time nor in harvesting.

Ernest Dowson.

THE MEMORIAL GARDEN

Half-sated with the petalled chalice fair,
Yet thieving still,
A roaming bee hums through the hot sweet air
To poise at will.

Behind the speckled laurel and dark box,
On either hand,
Crimson and golden-bright the hollyhocks
Like sentries stand.

And here, 'neath sweeping boughs, and shadow flung
And murm'rous sound,
A slender couch of twisted meshes hung
Just o'er the ground.

Within the swaying net-work thou wouldst lie
In ease serene:
Only a dome of leafy boughs on high,
With sky between.

Dear, thou hast found amid the happy dead
Shadow and rest;
And deeply sweet forgetfulness is shed
Upon thy breast.

For us the cares that vex, the footsteps sore,
The daily round,
For thee the stillness of the poppied shore
And sleep profound.

The fretful changes of the day renew
Their tedious flight,
Thine are the silences, the starry dew,
The tides of night.

Thine are the mysteries that darkness yields
To souls divine,
And the faint sweetnesses of dreaming fields
And flowers are thine.

ARTHUR CECIL HILLIER.

THE CAP AND BELLS

A QUEEN was beloved by a jester,
  And once when the owls grew still
He made his soul go upward
  And stand on her window sill.

In a long and straight blue garment,
  It talked before morn was white,
And it had grown wise by thinking
  Of a footfall hushed and light.

But the young queen would not listen;
  She rose in her pale night gown,
She drew in the brightening casement
  And pushed the brass bolt down.

He bade his heart go to her,
  When the bats cried out no more,
In a red and quivering garment
  It sang to her through the door,

The tongue of it sweet with dreaming
  Of a flutter of flower-like hair,
But she took up her fan from the table
  And waved it off on the air.

'I've cap and bell,' he pondered,
  'I will send them to her and die.'
And as soon as the morn had whitened
  He left them where she went by.

She laid them upon her bosom,
  Under a cloud of her hair,
And her red lips sang them a love song.
  The stars grew out of the air.

She opened her door and her window,
  And the heart and the soul came through,
To her right hand came the red one,
  To her left hand came the blue.

They set up a noise like crickets,
  A chattering wise and sweet,
And her hair was a folded flower,
  And the quiet of love in her feet.

W. B. Yeats.

THE COMING OF WAR

GATHER the people, for the battle breaks:
    From camping grounds above the valley,
Gather the men at arms, and bid them rally;
    Because the morn, the battle, wakes.
High throned above the mountains and the main,
Triumphs the sun! far down, the pasture plain
        To trampling armour shakes.

This was the meaning of those plenteous years,
    Those unarmed years of peace unbroken:
Flashing war crowns them! Now war's trump hath
    spoken
    Their final glory in our ears.
The old blood of our pastoral fathers now
Riots about our heart, and through our brow:
        Their sons can have no fears.

This was our whispering and haunting dream,
When cornlands flourished, red and golden;
When vines hung purple, nor could be withholden
The radiant outburst of their stream.
Earth cried to us, that all her laboured store
Was ours: that she had more to give, and more:
For nothing, did we deem?

We give her back the glory of this hour.
O sun and earth! O strength and beauty!
We use you now, we thank you now: our duty
We stand to do, mailed in your power.
A little people of a favoured land,
Helmed with the blessing of the morn we stand:
Our life is at its flower.

Gather the people, let the battle break:
An hundred peaceful years are over.
Now march each man to battle, as a lover:
For him, whom death shall overtake,
Sleeping upon this field, about his gloom
Voices shall pierce, to thrill his sacred tomb,
Of pride for his great sake.

With melody about us; heart and feet
Responding to one mighty measure:
Glad with the splendour of a sacred pleasure;

Swayed, one and all, as wind sways wheat:
Answering the sunlight with our eyes aglow,
Serene, and proud, and passionate, we go
Through airs of morning sweet.

Let no man dare to be disheartened now!
We challenge death beyond denial:
Against the host of death we make our trial:
Lord God of Hosts! do thou,
Who gavest us the fulness of thy sun
On fields of peace, perfect war's work begun:
Warriors, to thee we bow.

O life-blood of remembrance! Long ago
This land upheld our ancient fathers:
And for this land, their land, our land, now gathers
One fellowship against the foe.
The spears flash: be they as our mothers' eyes!
The trump sounds: hearken to our fathers' cries!
March we to battle so.

LIONEL JOHNSON.

LADY MACBETH

(For a Picture by John S. Sargent, A.R.A.)

O LET me plant my feet upon the ground
  More firmly; stand erect and meet the sway
  And surge of royal Fate, before it stay.
This is the poise of Time, whence what rebound
I know not; for within this golden round
  I hold above my hair, those splendours play
  Which, be they for an age or for a day,
Shall blaze or burn upon my forehead crowned.

Why pause, O Queen foredestined? 'tis the way
  To mar e'en Fate, untaken on the bound—
  Lives there from that dread night some shadow of sound
Within mine ear? or from some future fray
  The clash of arms, disaster's disarray?
  Or is't the drip of blood upon the ground?

G. A. GREENE.

TIME'S MONOTONE

AUTUMN and Winter,
Summer and Spring—
Hath time no other song to sing ?
Weary we grow of the changeless tune—
June and December,
December and June !

Time, like a bird, hath but one song,
One way to build, like a bird, hath he;
Thus hath he built so long, so long,
Thus hath he sung—ah me!

Time, like a spider, knows, be sure,
One only wile, though he seems so wise:
Death is his web, and Love his lure,
And you and I his flies.

'Love!' he sings
In the morning clear,
'Love! Love! Love!'
And you never hear

How under his breath
He whispers 'Death!
Death! Death!'

Yet Time—'tis the strangest thing of all—
Knoweth not the sense of the words he saith,
Eternity taught him his parrot-call
Of 'Love and Death.'

Year after year doth the old man climb
The mountainous knees of Eternity,
But Eternity telleth nothing to Time—
It may not be.

RICHARD LE GALLIENNE.

THE SHELLEY MEMORIAL

(*The Master's Speech*).

'The Rebel of eighty years ago
Is the Hero of to-day.'
In this memorial none will know
The Rebel of eighty years ago.
We Oxford Dons, however slow,
Are now at last compelled to say
'The Rebel of eighty years ago
Is the Hero of to-day.'

Ernest Radford.

THE WAIL OF THE DECADENT

Oh Heart of Man!
What ills torment, what passions tear
The heart of man!
The Muses gathered in a clan
All, all with sad consent, declare
The burden is too hard to bear,
Oh Heart of Man!

Ernest Radford.

THE OLD SHEPHERD

THE old, old, shepherd scarcely heeds,
  Crouched on his thin old hams;
Making a small red fire of reeds
  He turns his back on the lambs.

'My old, old shepherd, now beware,
  My young, young lambs will stray,
Where is your pipe, your pastoral air,
  Your songs, and your crook to-day?'

'My pipe is here, it warms my hands,
  No need of songs, or crooks.
I know the meadows, cliffs, and sands,
  I know the ponds and brooks.

'I only fear to need no fears,—
  Sheep go the old, old way.
I would give half my few cold years
  Just to see one lamb stray.'

At night returned with peaceful mind,
'Here are your flocks,' he said,
But the wolf had smelt that his eyes were blind,
The crow, that my sheep were dead.

EDWIN J. ELLIS.

MIDSUMMER DAY

PALE, pure and lucent, o'er the quiet fields
The purple twilight with its one white star
Melts to the very heart of heaven afar,
And hardly to the summer darkness yields.

The dim white road like something ghostly leads
Through trees that plead the majesty of time,
And heard, I doubt not, in their leafy prime,
Of green Savannah-worlds and Raleigh's deeds.

In this deep quietude all things are blest
Through tender dimness of the earth and sky :
Save for a swallow's melancholy cry—
All things at last are still and all have rest.

And yet beneath this twilight soft and bland
The labyrinthine ways of London spread :
The streets a million weary footsteps tread
From suburb brickfields to the roaring Strand.

ARTHUR CECIL HILLIER.

Ah, dans ces mornes séjours
Les jamais sont les toujours.

Paul Verlaine.

You would have understood me, had you waited ;
I could have loved you, dear ! as well as he :
Had we not been impatient, dear ! and fated
Always to disagree.

What is the use of speech ? Silence were fitter :
Lest we should still be wishing things unsaid.
Though all the words we ever spake were bitter,
Shall I reproach you dead ?

Nay, let this earth, your portion, likewise cover
All the old anger, setting us apart :
Always, in all, in truth was I your lover;
Always, I held your heart.

I have met other women who were tender,
As you were cold, dear ! with a grace as rare.
Think you, I turned to them, or made surrender,
I who had found you fair ?

Had we been patient, dear! ah, had you waited,
    I had fought death for you, better than he:
But from the very first, dear! we were fated
        Always to disagree.

Late, late, I come to you, now death discloses
    Love that in life was not to be our part:
On your low lying mound between the roses,
        Sadly I cast my heart.

I would not waken you: nay! this is fitter;
    Death and the darkness give you unto me;
Here we who loved so, were so cold and bitter,
        Hardly can disagree.

ERNEST DOWSON.

ON GREAT SUGARLOAF

WHERE Sugarloaf with bare and ruinous wedge
  Cleaves the grey air to view the darkening sea,
  We stood on high, and heard the northwind flee
Through clouds storm-heavy fallen from ledge to ledge.

Then sudden 'Look !' we cried. The far black edge
  Of south horizon oped in sunbright glee,
  And a broad water shone, one moment free,
Ere darkness veiled again the wavering sedge.

Such is the Poet's inspiration, still
  Too evanescent ! coming but to go :
  Such the great passions shewing good in ill,

Quick brightnesses, love-lights too soon burnt low :
  And such Man's life, while flashes Heaven's will,
  Between two glooms a transitory glow.

G. A. GREENE.

CELTIC SPEECH

NEVER forgetful silence fall on thee,
  Nor younger voices overtake thee,
Nor echoes from thine ancient hills forsake thee,
  Old music heard by Mona of the Sea:
And where with moving melodies there break thee
  Pastoral Conway, venerable Dee.

Like music lives, nor may that music die,
  Still in the far, fair Gaelic places:
The speech, so wistful with its kindly graces,
  Holy Croagh Patrick knows, and holy Hy:
The speech, that wakes the soul in withered faces,
  And wakes remembrance of great things gone by.

Like music by the desolate Land's End,
  Mournful forgetfulness hath broken:
No more words kindred to the winds are spoken,
  Where upon iron cliffs whole seas expend
That strength, whereof the unalterable token
  Remains wild music, even to the world's end.

LIONEL JOHNSON.

THE NIGHT-JAR*

On the river, in the shallows, on the shore,
  Are the darkness and the silence of the tomb;
O'er the woods the sunset tinged an hour before
      Utter gloom.

'Twixt the ramparts of the mighty aspen trees,
  In midstream, the pallid waters gleam afar, .
Not a ripple on their surface, not a breeze,
      Not a star.

Where the shadow of the ruined water-mill
  Hides the mill-pool and its anchored lily fleet,
And the warm air seems to slumber over-still,
      Over-sweet,

Hark the Night-jar! In the meadows by the stream
  Sounds the bird's unearthly note: I like it well,
For it lulls you as the mystery of a dream,
      Or a spell.

* 'They are the witches among birds.'

All the nightingales along the bowery reach
  Plain together when the midnight moon is bright:
This bird only knows by heart the secret speech
      Of dark night.

Turn the boat now! row away, friends; let us hence,
  Lest the glamour of the night's o'er-trancing breath
Plunge us one and all into that dream intense
      Which is Death!

VICTOR PLARR.

THE SONG OF THE OLD MOTHER

I RISE in the dawn, and I kneel and blow
Till the seed of the fire flicker and glow.
And then I must scrub, and bake, and sweep,
Till stars are beginning to blink and peep,
But the young lie long and dream in their bed
Of the matching of ribbons, the blue and the red,
And their day goes over in idleness,
And they sigh if the wind but lift up a tress.
While I must work, because I am old
And the seed of the fire gets feeble and cold.

W. B. YEATS.

THE FIRST SPRING DAY

Yes it is Spring's
First breath! O the soft wind
That, ranging through my garden solitude
Upon his murmuring wings,
Wakes in all tender things
The bliss of life renewed!

Somewhere, I know,
The lark's wild ecstasy
Is shaking the blue sky,
Though winter's latest snow
In far-off crannies of the purple hill,
By noon untrodden, still
Lingering may lie.

For March, the churl, this one sweet day,
Smiles at my window from the South,
As though the virgin kiss of new-born May
Were warm upon his mouth.

He woos me to look out and see
  How the bright sun
Sets budding every tree,
  And wakes the flowers each one.
Crocuses peering up,
Joy in each golden cup,
  Say: 'Winter's reign is done!'
And in my orchard-close the sweet birds sing:
    'No more Winter is king,
Open your windows, and let in the Spring!'

JOHN TODHUNTER.

AN ODE TO SPRING

Is it the Spring ?
  Or are the birds all wrong,
That play on flute and viol,
  A thousand strong,
In minstrel galleries
  Of the long deep wood,
Epiphanies
  Of bloom and bud.

Grave minstrels those,
  Of deep responsive chant;
But see how yonder goes,
  Dew-drunk, with giddy slant,
Yon Shelley-lark
  And hark !
Him on the giddy brink
  Of pearly Heaven
His fairy anvil clink

Or watch, in fancy,
  How the brimming note
Falls like a string of pearls
  From out his heavenly throat;
Or like a fountain
  In Hesperides,
Raining its silver rain,
  In gleam and chime,
On backs of ivory girls—
  Twice happy rhyme!—
Ah, none of these
  May make it plain,
No image we may seek
Shall match the magic of his gurgling beak.

And many a silly thing
  That hops and cheeps,
And perks his tiny tail,
  And sideway peeps,
And flutters little wing,
  Seems in his consequential way
To tell of Spring.

The river warbles soft and runs
  With fuller curve and sleeker line,
Though on the winter-blackened hedge
  Twigs of unbudding iron shine,
And trampled still the river-sedge.

And O the Sun!
I have no friend so generous as this Sun
That comes to meet me with his big warm hands.
And O the Sky!
There is no maid, how true,
Is half so chaste
As the pure kiss of greening willow wands
Against the intense pale blue
Of this sweet boundless over-arching waste.

And see!—dear Heaven, but it is the Spring!—
  See yonder, yonder, by the river there,
Long glittering pearly fingers flash
  Upon the warm bright air:
Why 'tis the heavenly palm,
  The Christian tree,
Whose budding is a psalm
  Of natural piety;
Soft silver notches up the smooth green stem,
  Ah, Spring must follow them,
It is the Spring!

O spirit of Spring,
  Whose strange instinctive art
Makes the bird sing,
  And brings the bud again;
O in my heart
  Take up thy heavenly reign,

And from its deeps
  Draw out the hidden flower,
And where it sleeps,
  Throughout the winter long,
O sweet mysterious power,
  Awake the slothful song!

RICHARD LE GALLIENNE.

A PRESIDING EXAMINER

EMERGING from the darkness
Of London's sullen frown,
I simulating Majesty
Appeared in hood and gown,

Commissioned to examine,
According to the rule,
In all that they could cram in,
The boys of my old school.

* * * *

I sat in my imposing seat:
The papers from me flew
As though my learning were complete,
And I all knowledge knew.

But O! despite the hood and gown,
Despite the high respect
Paid to a mild official frown,
Yet had I to reflect

That 'neath a borrowed mortar-board
Mere ghosts of knowledge dwelt;
That false was my pretended hoard:
Ah me, how poor I felt!

Ah boys, despite my college,
I am a learnèd man:
I've loads of sorry knowledge
Not set in any plan.

My wisdom hard in earning
I'd give it all to know
Again what I was learning
Now twenty years ago.

ERNEST RADFORD.

A RHYME ON RHYME

WHO made first our words resemble
With division and with tremble,
Saving them from song's perdition
The abyss of repetition,
And gave the flower of rhyme from earth to air for air's
fruition?

Did he measure all the meaning
Of the rhymes he left for gleaning
In the dancing hand and hand?
Did he know the joyous band?
Did he see the singing sisters, did he love and under-
stand?

There was no such old Magician.
The blind murmurs of Tradition
Dimly shaped and never knew
Of those sounds so sweet and few
That make metre all one vessel and her singers all one
crew.

Music pouring from the boundless
Sheds her life upon the soundless.
Pretty rhyme, while doves are cooing,
Looking down on lovers wooing,
Adds the sisterhood of saying to the brotherhood of
doing.

EDWIN J. ELLIS.

List of Books

in

Belles Lettres

ALL THE BOOKS IN THIS CATALOGUE ARE PUBLISHED AT NET PRICES.

1894

Telegraphic Address—
'BODLEIAN, LONDON.'

'A WORD must be said for the manner in which the publishers have produced the volume (*i.e.*, "The Earth Fiend"), a sumptuous folio, printed by CONSTABLE, the etchings on Japanese paper by MR. GOULDING. The volume should add not only to MR. STRANG'S fame but to that of MESSRS. ELKIN MATHEWS AND JOHN LANE, who are rapidly gaining distinction for their beautiful editions of belles-lettres.'—*Daily Chronicle*, Sept. 24, 1892.

Referring to MR. LE GALLIENNE'S 'English Poems' *and* 'Silhouettes' by MR. ARTHUR SYMONS:—'We only refer to them now to note a fact which they illustrate, and which we have been observing of late, namely, the recovery to a certain extent of good taste in the matter of printing and binding books. These two books, which are turned out by MESSRS. ELKIN MATHEWS AND JOHN LANE, are models of artistic publishing, and yet they are simplicity itself. The books with their excellent printing and their very simplicity make a harmony which is satisfying to the artistic sense.'—*Sunday Sun*, Oct. 2, 1892.

'MR. LE GALLIENNE is a fortunate young gentleman. I don't know by what legerdemain he and his publishers work, but here, in an age as stony to poetry as the ages of Chatterton and Richard Savage, we find the full edition of his book sold before publication. How is it done, MESSRS. ELKIN MATHEWS AND JOHN LANE? for, without depreciating MR. LE GALLIENNE'S sweetness and charm, I doubt that the marvel would have been wrought under another publisher. These publishers, indeed, produce books so delightfully, that it must give an added pleasure to the hoarding of first editions.'—KATHARINE TYNAN in *The Irish Daily Independent.*

'To MESSRS. ELKIN MATHEWS AND JOHN LANE almost more than to any other, we take it, are the thanks of the grateful singer especially due; for it is they who have managed, by means of limited editions and charming workmanship, to impress book-buyers with the belief that a volume may have an æsthetic and commercial value. They have made it possible to speculate in the latest discovered poet, as in a new company—with the difference that an operation in the former can be done with three half-crowns.'—*St. James's Gazette.*

List of Books

IN

BELLES LETTRES

(Including some Transfers)

PUBLISHED BY

Elkin Mathews & John Lane

The Bodley Head

VIGO STREET, LONDON, W.

N.B.—The Authors and Publishers reserve the right of reprinting any book in this list if a new Edition is called for, except in cases where a stipulation has been made to the contrary, and of printing a separate edition of any of the books for America irrespective of the numbers to which the English editions are limited. The numbers mentioned do not include the copies sent for review, nor those supplied to the public libraries.

ADAMS (FRANCIS).

ESSAYS IN MODERNITY. cr. 8vo. 5*s. net.*
[*In preparation.*

ALLEN (GRANT).

THE LOWER SLOPES: A VOLUME OF VERSE, with title page and cover design by J. ILLINGWORTH KAY. 600 copies, cr. 8vo. 5*s. net.*

ANTÆUS.

THE BACKSLIDER, AND OTHER POEMS. 100 only, sm. 4to. 7*s.* 6*d. net.* [*Very few remain.*

BENSON (EUGENE).

FROM THE ASOLAN HILLS. A Poem. 300 copies, imp. 16mo. 5*s. net.* [*Very few remain.*

BINYON (LAURENCE).

LYRIC POEMS, with title page by SELWYN IMAGE. Sq. 16mo. 5*s. net.*

BOURDILLON (F. W.).

A LOST GOD. A Poem, with Illustrations by H. J. FORD. 500 copies, 8vo. 6*s. net.* [*Very few remain.*

CHAPMAN (ELIZABETH RACHEL).

A LITTLE CHILD'S WREATH: A Sonnet Sequence. 350 copies. Sq. 16mo. 3*s.* 6*d. net.*

COLERIDGE (HON. STEPHEN).

THE SANCTITY OF CONFESSION. A Romance. 2nd edition, cr. 8vo. 3*s. net.* [*A few remain.*

CRANE (WALTER).

RENASCENCE. A Book of Verse. Frontispiece and 38 designs by the Author. [*Small paper edition out of print.* There remain a few large paper copies, fcap. 4to. £1. 1*s. net.* And a few fcap. 4to. Japanese vellum. £1. 15*s. net.*

CROSSING (WM.)

THE ANCIENT CROSSES OF DARTMOOR. With 11 plates, 8vo. cloth. 4*s.* 6*d. net.* [*Very few remain.*

DAVIDSON (JOHN).

PLAYS: An Unhistorical Pastoral; A Romantic Farce; Bruce, a Chronicle Play; Smith, a Tragic Farce; Scaramouch in Naxos, a Pantomime, with a frontispiece and cover design by AUBREY BEARDSLEY. 500 copies. Small 4to. 7*s.* 6*d. net.*

DAVIDSON (JOHN).

THE NORTH WALL. Fcap. 8vo. 2*s.* 6*d. net.* [*Very few remain.*

Transferred by the Author to the present Publishers.

DAVIDSON (JOHN).

FLEET STREET ECLOGUES. 2nd edition, fcap. 8vo. buckram. 5*s. net.*

DAVIDSON (JOHN).

A RANDOM ITINERARY: Prose Sketches, with a Ballad. Frontispiece, title page, and cover design by LAURENCE HOUSMAN. 600 copies. Fcap. 8vo., Irish linen. 5*s. net.*

DE GRUCHY (AUGUSTA).

UNDER THE HAWTHORN, AND OTHER VERSES. *Frontispiece by Walter Crane.* 300 copies, cr. 8vo. 5*s. net.* Also 30 copies on Japanese vellum. 15*s. net.* [*Very few remain.*

DE TABLEY (LORD).

POEMS, DRAMATIC AND LYRICAL. By JOHN LEICESTER WARREN (Lord De Tabley), illustrations and cover design by C. S. RICKETTS. 2nd edition, cr. 8vo. 7*s.* 6*d. net.*

FIELD (MICHAEL).

SIGHT AND SONG (Poems on Pictures). 400 copies, fcap. 8vo. 5*s. net.* [*Very few remain.*

FIELD (MICHAEL).

STEPHANIA: A TRIALOGUE IN 3 ACTS. 250 copies, pott 4to. 6*s. net.* [*Very few remain.*

GALE (NORMAN).

ORCHARD SONGS, with title page and cover design by J. ILLINGWORTH KAY. Fcap. 8vo., Irish linen. 5*s. net.*
Also a special edition, limited in number, on hand-made paper, bound in English vellum. £1. 1*s. net.*

GARNETT (RICHARD).

POEMS, with title page designed by J. ILLINGWORTH KAY. 350 copies, cr. 8vo. 5*s. net.*

GOSSE (EDMUND).

THE LETTERS OF THOMAS LOVELL BEDDOES. Now first edited. Pott 8vo. 5*s. net.*

GRAHAME (KENNETH).

PAGAN PAPERS: A VOLUME OF ESSAYS, with title page by AUBREY BEARDSLEY. Fcap. 8vo. 5*s. net.*

GREENE (G. A.).

ITALIAN LYRISTS OF TO-DAY. Translations in the original metres from about 35 living Italian poets; with bibliographical and biographical notes, cr. 8vo. 5*s. net.*

HAKE (DR. T. GORDON).

A SELECTION FROM HIS POEMS. Edited by Mrs. MEYNELL, with a portrait after D. G. ROSSETTI, and a cover design by GLEESON WHITE. Cr. 8vo. 5*s. net.*

HALLAM (ARTHUR HENRY).

THE POEMS, together with his Essay "On some of the Characteristics of Modern Poetry and on the Lyrical Poems of Alfred Tennyson." Edited, with an introduction, by RICHARD LE GALLIENNE, 550 copies, fcap. 8vo. 5*s. net.* [*Very few remain.*

HAMILTON (COL. IAN).

THE BALLAD OF HADJI, AND OTHER POEMS. Etched frontispiece by WM. STRANG. 550 copies, fcap. 8vo. 3*s. net.*

Transferred by the Author to the present Publishers.

HAZLITT (WILLIAM).

LIBER AMORIS: a reprint of the 1823 edition, with numerous original documents appended, never before printed, including MRS. HAZLITT's Diary in Scotland; Portrait after BEWICK; Facsimile Letters, &c.; and the critical introduction by RICHARD LE GALLIENNE prefixed to the edition of 1893. 400 copies. 4to., green buckram. £1. 1*s. net.* [*Very shortly.*

HICKEY (EMILY H.).

VERSE TALES, LYRICS, AND TRANSLATIONS. 300 copies, imp. 16mo. 5*s. net.*

HORNE (HERBERT P.).

DIVERSI COLORES. Poems with ornaments by the Author, 250 copies, 16mo. 5*s.* *net.*

JAMES (W. P.).

ROMANTIC PROFESSIONS: A VOLUME OF ESSAYS. With title page by J. ILLINGWORTH KAY. 450 copies. Cr. 8vo., buckram. 5*s.* *net.*

JOHNSON (EFFIE).

IN THE FIRE, AND OTHER FANCIES. Frontispiece by WALTER CRANE. 500 copies, imp. 16mo. 3*s.* 6*d.* *net.*

JOHNSON (LIONEL).

THE ART OF THOMAS HARDY. Six Essays, with etched portrait by WM. STRANG, and bibliography by JOHN LANE, cr. 8vo. 5*s.* 6*d.* *net.*

Also 150 copies, large paper, with proofs of the portrait. £1. 1*s.* *net.* [*Very Shortly.*

JOHNSON (LIONEL).

A VOLUME OF POEMS, fcap. 8vo. 5*s.* *net.* [*In preparation.*

KEATS (JOHN).

THREE ESSAYS, now issued in book form for the first time. Edited by H. BUXTON FORMAN, with life mask by HAYDON. Fcap. 4to. 10*s.* 6*d.* *net.* [*Very few remain.*

KEYNOTES SERIES.

Each Volume with specially-designed title page by AUBREY BEARDSLEY, cr. 8vo., cloth. 3*s.* 6*d.* *net.*

Vol. I. KEYNOTES, by GEORGE EGERTON. [*Fourth Edition now ready.*

Vol. II. THE DANCING FAUN, by FLORENCE FARR.

Vol. III. POOR FOLK. Translated from the Russian of F. DOSTOIEVSKY, by LENA MILMAN, with a preface by GEORGE MOORE.

Vol. IV. A CHILD OF THE AGE, by FRANCIS ADAMS. [*In rapid preparation*

Vol. V. THE GREAT GOD PAN AND THE INMOST LIGHT, by ARTHUR MACHEN. [*In preparation.*

LEATHER (R. K.).

VERSES. 250 copies, fcap. 8vo. 3s. *net.*
Transferred by the Author to the present Publishers.

LEATHER (R. K.), & RICHARD LE GALLIENNE.

THE STUDENT AND THE BODY-SNATCHER, AND OTHER TRIFLES. [*Small paper edition out of print.* There remain a very few of the 50 large paper copies. 7s. 6d. *net.*

LE GALLIENNE (RICHARD).

PROSE FANCIES, with a portrait of the Author, by WILSON STEER. Crown 8vo., purple cloth, uniform with "THE RELIGION OF A LITERARY MAN." 5s. *net.* Also a limited large paper edition. 8vo. 12s. 6d. *net.* [*Immediately.*

LE GALLIENNE (RICHARD).

THE BOOK BILLS OF NARCISSUS. An account rendered by RICHARD LE GALLIENNE. 2nd edition, cr. 8vo., buckram. 3s. 6d. *net.*

LE GALLIENNE (RICHARD).

ENGLISH POEMS. 3rd edition, cr. 8vo., purple cloth, uniform with "THE RELIGION OF A LITERARY MAN." 5s. *net.*

LE GALLIENNE (RICHARD).

GEORGE MEREDITH: Some Characteristics; with a Bibliography (much enlarged) by JOHN LANE, portrait, &c. 3rd edition, cr. 8vo. 5s. 6d. *net.*

LE GALLIENNE (RICHARD).

THE RELIGION OF A LITERARY MAN. 4th thousand. Cr. 8vo., purple cloth. 3s. 6d. *net.* Also a special rubricated edition on hand-made paper. 8vo. 10s. 6d. *net.*

LETTERS TO LIVING ARTISTS.

500 copies, fcap. 8vo. 3s. 6d. *net.* [*Very few remain.*

MARSTON (PHILIP BOURKE).

A LAST HARVEST: LYRICS AND SONNETS FROM THE BOOK OF LOVE. Edited by LOUISE CHANDLER MOULTON. 500 copies, fcap. 8vo. 5*s*. *net*.
Also 50 copies on large paper, hand-made. 10*s*. 6*d*. *net*.
[*Very few remain.*

MARTIN (W. WILSEY).

QUATRAINS, LIFE'S MYSTERY, AND OTHER POEMS. 16mo. 2*s*. 6*d*. *net*. [*Very few remain.*

MARZIALS (THEO.).

THE GALLERY OF PIGEONS, AND OTHER POEMS. Fcap. 8vo. 4*s*. 6*d*. *net*. [*Very few remain.*
Transferred by the Author to the present Publishers.

MEYNELL (MRS.) (ALICE C. THOMPSON).

POEMS. 2nd edition, fcap. 8vo. 3*s*. 6*d*. *net*. A few of the 50 large paper copies (1st edition) remain. 12*s*. 6*d*. *net*.

MEYNELL (MRS.).

THE RHYTHM OF LIFE, AND OTHER ESSAYS. 2nd Edition, fcap. 8vo. 3*s*. 6*d*. *net*. A few of the 50 large paper copies (1st edition) remain. 12*s*. 6*d*. *net*.

MONKHOUSE (ALLAN).

BOOKS AND PLAYS: a Volume of Essays. 400 copies. crown 8vo. 5*s*. *net*. [*Immediately.*

MURRAY (ALMA).

PORTRAIT AS BEATRICE CENCI. With critical notice, containing four letters from ROBERT BROWNING. 8vo. wrapper. 2*s*. *net*.

NETTLESHIP (J. T.).

ROBERT BROWNING. Essays and Thoughts. Third edition, cr. 8vo. 5*s*. 6*d*. *net*. *In preparation*. Half a dozen of the Whatman L.P. copies (first edition) remain. £1. 1*s*. *net*.

NOBLE (JAS. ASHCROFT).

THE SONNET IN ENGLAND, AND OTHER ESSAYS. Title-page and cover design by AUSTIN YOUNG. 600 copies. cr. 8vo. 5*s. net.*
Also 50 copies L.P. 12*s.* 6*d. net.*

NOEL (HON. RODEN).

POOR PEOPLE'S CHRISTMAS. 250 copies. 16mo. 1*s. net.*
[*Very few remain.*

OXFORD CHARACTERS.

A series of lithographed portraits by WILL ROTHENSTEIN, with text by F. YORK POWELL and others. To be issued monthly in term. Each part will contain two portraits. Parts I. to V. ready, 200 sets only, folio, wrapper. 5*s. net* per part. Also 25 special large paper sets, containing proofs of the portraits, signed by the artist. 10*s.* 6*d. net* per part.

PINKERTON (PERCY).

GALEAZZO : a Venetian Episode, and other Poems. Etched frontispiece. 16mo. 5*s. net.* [*Very few remain.*
Transferred by the Author to the present Publishers.

RADFORD (DOLLIE).

SONGS. A new volume of verse. [*In preparation.*

RADFORD (ERNEST).

CHAMBERS TWAIN. Frontispiece by WALTER CRANE. 250 copies. Imp. 16mo. 5*s. net.*
Also 50 copies large paper. 10*s.* 6*d. net.* [*Very few remain.*

RHYMERS' CLUB, THE SECOND BOOK OF THE.

With contributions by E. DOWSON, E. J. ELLIS, G. A. GREENE, A. HILLIER, L. JOHNSON, R. LE GALLIENNE, V. PLARR, E. RADFORD, E. RHYS, T. W. ROLLESTON, A. SYMONS, J. TODHUNTER, and W. B. YEATS. 500 copies (400 for sale). Sq. 16mo. 5*s. net.* Also 50 copies large paper, 10*s.* 6*d. net.* [*Immediately.*

RHYS (ERNEST).

A LONDON ROSE, AND OTHER RHYMES, with title page designed by SELWYN IMAGE. 350 copies, cr. 8vo., 5*s. net.*

RICKETTS (C. S.) and C. H. SHANNON.

HERO AND LEANDER. By CHRISTOPHER MARLOWE and GEORGE CHAPMAN, with borders, initials, and illustrations designed and engraved on the wood by C. S. RICKETTS and C. H. SHANNON. Bound in English vellum and gold. 200 copies only. 35*s. net.*

SCHAFF (DR. P.).

LITERATURE AND POETRY: Papers on Dante, etc. Portrait and Plates. 100 copies only. 8vo. 10*s. net.*

STODDARD (R. H.).

THE LION'S CUB: WITH OTHER VERSE. Portrait. 100 copies only, bound in an illuminated Persian design. Fcap. 8vo. 5*s. net.* [*Very few remain.*

STREET (G. S.).

THE AUTOBIOGRAPHY OF A BOY. Passages selected by his friend G. S. S., with title page designed by C. W. FURSE. 500 copies, fcap. 8vo. 3*s.* 6*d. net.*

SYMONDS (JOHN ADDINGTON).

IN THE KEY OF BLUE, AND OTHER PROSE ESSAYS. Cover design by C. S. RICKETTS. 2nd edition, thick cr. 8vo. 8*s.* 6*d. net.*

THOMPSON (FRANCIS).

A VOLUME OF POEMS. With frontispiece, title page, and cover design by LAURENCE HOUSMAN. 4th edition, pott 4to. 5*s. net.*

TODHUNTER (JOHN).

A SICILIAN IDYLL. Frontispiece by WALTER CRANE. 250 copies. Imp. 16mo. 5*s. net.*

Also 50 copies on hand-made large paper, fcap. 4to. 10*s.* 6*d. net.* [*Very few remain.*

TOMSON (GRAHAM R.).

AFTER SUNSET. A volume of Poems. With title page and cover design by R. ANNING BELL. Fcap. 8vo. 5*s. net.*
Also a limited large paper edition. 12*s.* 6*d. net.*

[*In preparation.*

TREE (H. BEERBOHM).

THE IMAGINATIVE FACULTY. A Lecture delivered at the Royal Institution. With portrait of MR. TREE from an unpublished drawing by the MARCHIONESS OF GRANBY. Fcap. 8vo., boards. 2*s.* 6*d. net.*

TYNAN HINKSON (KATHARINE).

CUCKOO SONGS. With title page and cover design by LAURENCE HOUSMAN. 500 copies, fcap. 8vo. 5*s. net.*

VAN DYKE (HENRY).

THE POETRY OF TENNYSON. 3rd edition, enlarged, cr. 8vo. 5*s.* 6*d. net.*

The late Laureate himself gave valuable aid in correcting various details.

WATSON (WILLIAM).

THE ELOPING ANGELS: A CAPRICE. Second edition, sq. 16mo. buckram. 3*s.* 6*d. net.*

WATSON (WILLIAM).

EXCURSIONS IN CRITICISM: BEING SOME PROSE RECREATIONS OF A RHYMER. 2nd edition, cr. 8vo. 5*s. net.*

WATSON (WILLIAM).

THE PRINCE'S QUEST, AND OTHER POEMS. With a bibliographical note added. 2nd edition, fcap. 8vo. 4*s.* 6*d. net.*

WEDMORE (FREDERICK).

PASTORALS OF FRANCE—RENUNCIATIONS. A volume of Stories. Title-page by JOHN FULLEYLOVE, R.I. 3rd edition, cr. 8vo. 5*s. net.*

A few of the large paper copies of Renunciations (1st Edition) remain. 10*s.* 6*d. net.*

WICKSTEED (P. H.).

DANTE: SIX SERMONS. 3rd edition, cr. 8vo. 2*s. net.*

WILDE (OSCAR).

THE SPHINX. A poem decorated throughout in line and colour, and bound in a design by CHARLES RICKETTS. 250 copies. £2. 2*s*. *net*. 25 copies large paper. £5. 5*s*. *net*.

WILDE (OSCAR).

The incomparable and ingenious history of Mr. W. H., being the true secret of Shakespear's sonnets now for the first time here fully set forth, with initial letters and cover design by CHARLES RICKETTS. 500 copies. 10*s*. 6*d*. *net*. Also 50 copies large paper. 21*s*. *net*.
[*In preparation*.

WILDE (OSCAR).

DRAMATIC WORKS, now printed for the first time with a specially designed binding to each volume by CHARLES SHANNON. 500 copies, sm. 4to. 7*s*. 6*d*. *net* per vol. Also 50 copies large paper. 15*s*. *net* per vol.

Vol. I. LADY WINDERMERE'S FAN. A comedy in four acts.

Vol. II. A WOMAN OF NO IMPORTANCE. A comedy in four acts. [*Immediately*.

Vol. III. THE DUCHESS OF PADUA. A blank verse tragedy in five acts. [*Shortly*.

WILDE (OSCAR).

SALOME. A Tragedy in one Act, done into English, with title page, 10 illustrations, tail piece, and cover design by AUBREY BEARDSLEY. 500 copies, sm. 4to. 15*s*. *net*. Also 100 copies large paper. 30*s*. *net*.

WYNNE (FRANCES).

WHISPER. A volume of Verse. Fcap. 8vo. 2*s*. 6*d*. *net*.

Transferred by the Author to the present Publishers.

A Memoir by KATHARINE TYNAN, and a portrait, have been added.

The Hobby Horse

A new series of this illustrated magazine will be published quarterly by subscription, under the Editorship of HERBERT P. HORNE. Subscription £1 per annum, post free, for the four numbers. Quarto, printed on hand-made paper, and issued in a limited edition to subscribers only. The Magazine will contain articles upon Literature, Music, Painting, Sculpture, Architecture, and the Decorative Arts; Poems; Essays; Fiction; original Designs; with reproductions of pictures and drawings by the old masters and contemporary artists. There will be a new title-page and ornaments designed by the Editor.

Among the contributors to the Hobby Horse are:

The late MATTHEW ARNOLD.
LAURENCE BINYON.
WILFRID BLUNT.
FORD MADOX BROWN.
The late ARTHUR BURGESS.
E. BURNE-JONES, A.R.A.
AUSTIN DOBSON.
RICHARD GARNETT, LL.D.
A. J. HIPKINS, F.S.A.
SELWYN IMAGE.
LIONEL JOHNSON.
RICHARD LE GALLIENNE.
SIR F. LEIGHTON, Bart., P.R.A.
T. HOPE MCLACHLAN.
MAY MORRIS.
C. HUBERT H. PARRY, Mus. Doc.
A. W. POLLARD.
F. YORK POWELL.
CHRISTINA G. ROSSETTI.
W. M. ROSSETTI.
JOHN RUSKIN, D.C.L., LL.D.
FREDERICK SANDYS.
The late W. BELL SCOTT.
FREDERICK J. SHIELDS.
J. H. SHORTHOUSE.
The late JAMES SMETHAM.
SIMEON SOLOMON.
A. SOMERVELL.
The late J. ADDINGTON SYMONDS.
KATHARINE TYNAN.
G. F. WATTS, R.A.
FREDERICK WEDMORE.
OSCAR WILDE.

Prospectuses on Application.

'Nearly every book put out by Messrs. Elkin Mathews and John Lane, at the Sign of the Bodley Head, is a satisfaction to the special senses of the modern bookman, for bindings, shapes, types, and papers. They have surpassed themselves, and registered a real achievement in English bookmaking by the volume of "Poems, Dramatic and Lyrical," of Lord De Tabley.'

Newcastle Daily Chronicle.

'A ray of hopefulness is stealing again into English poetry after the twilight greys of Clough, Arnold, and Tennyson. Even unbelief wears braver colours. Despite the jeremiads, which are the dirges of the elder gods, England is still a nest of singing-birds (*teste* the Catalogue of Elkin Mathews and John Lane).'—MR. ZANGWILL, in *Pall Mall Magazine.*

'One can nearly always be certain, when one sees on the title-page of any given book the name of Messrs. Elkin Mathews and John Lane as being the publishers thereof, that there will be something worth reading to be found between the boards.'—*World.*

'All Messrs. Mathews and Lane's books are so beautifully printed and so tastefully issued, that it rejoices the heart of a book-lover to handle them; but they have shewn their sound judgment not less markedly in the literary quality of their publications. The choiceness of form is not inappropriate to the matter, which is always of something more than ephemeral worth. This was a distinction on which the better publishers at one time prided themselves; they never lent their names to trash; but some names associated with worthy traditions have proved more than once a delusion and a snare. The record of Messrs. Elkin Mathews and John Lane is perfect in this respect, and their imprint is a guarantee of the worth of what they publish.'—*Birmingham Daily Post, Nov. 6th*, 1893.

www.ingramcontent.com/pod-product-compliance
Lightning Source LLC
Chambersburg PA
CBHW020557270326
41927CB00006B/884

* 9 7 8 3 3 3 7 2 5 9 4 1 9 *